THE SUBTLE ART OF *Fart Remarks*

Clever Things to Say When You Fart

Bree Kingwind

Illustrations by Mike Beck

Ulysses Press

Published in the United States by:
Ulysses Press
P.O. Box 3440
Berkeley, CA 94703
www.ulyssespress.com

ISBN: 978-1-61243-896-2
Library of Congress Catalog Number: 2018967988

Printed in the United States by Versa Press
10 9 8 7 6 5 4 3 2 1

Acquisitions: Bridget Thoreson
Managing editor: Claire Chun
Copyeditor: Lauren Harrison
Proofreader: Renee Rutledge
Cover design: Ashley Prine
Cover artwork: background © Katrien1/shutterstock.com
Interior design: what!design @ whatweb.com

Distributed by Publishers Group West

Introduction

Fart, toot, cut the cheese, or bottom blast–whatever you call it, we all do it. Yes, we ALL fart. Everyone from your Uncle Phil to the Queen of England. Farts are a noisy, smelly fact of life. Which brings us to the age-old questions: What do you say when you do it? Do you keep mum and act innocent as everyone crinkles up their noses? Or do you fess up? And if you fess up, what can you say to clear the air?

Well, friends, there's a subtle art to "fart remarks," those witty or not-so-witty things you say when you pass gas, and this book will teach you all of them. Whether you want to own or disown that cloud of methane, we've got all the re(butt)als for the sounds and smells that come out of your butt.

The Fart Chart

Farts come in all shapes and sizes, or should we say sharts and stench clouds, so let's start by defining the essential fart types.

THE DUCK CALL

This flurry of flatulence is your classic "PFFFFFFFFFFFFFFTPT" noise maker. It can be smelly or odorless, but either way, you'll grab the attention of anyone in your vicinity, so arm yourself with the perfect fart remark.

BUTT PUTT

This pop, pop, pop type of fart sounds like a machine gun and its stench is just as deadly.

GIGGLE GAS

Just like the punchline of that joke, you didn't see this one coming. It's that quick quack you let out when a giggle jiggles just a little too hard.

SPHINCTER WHISTLE
Like a deflating balloon or a single-note trombone,
this type of fart is music to our ears and rears.

GRUNDLE RUMBLE
It's silent but surely deadly and definitely packing heat.
Like an ass-ass-in, you're never really sure if you can trust
it. Is it pure gas or something more?

HINEY HOWL
This one may howl like your dog and the smell
sure bites like him too!

THE SHART SURPRISE
This is why you have trust issues. This one could have gone
one of two ways, and to your surprise, it went the #2 way.

GUT GRENADE
This is the one that didn't get away. All of your attempts
to hold in a major honker and it backfires, literally. You get
the same embarrassing sound but none of the relief.

In an
Apple store

OWN IT:

It's not my fault there are
no Windows in here!

When you're a generally polite person who owns up to their farts

OWN IT:

Excuse me!

In Australia

OWN IT:

There's a thunder down under!

In a cemetery

OWN IT:

I'm being haunted by the ghost
of that burrito I had for lunch!

In Italy

DISOWN IT:

Non ero io a fare quel puzzo.

OWN IT:

I am Farticus!

In the '70s

DISOWN IT:

That's sick! Who laid a gasser?

OWN IT:

I laid a wicked gasser!

16

In the '80s

DISOWN IT:

Ugh! Gag me out the door!
Who farted?

In the '90s

DISOWN IT:

Me? Fart? As if!

When you're Harry Potter

OWN IT:

Unexpecto fartronum!

When you're a silent but deadly farter

DISOWN IT:

Say nothing. People might suspect you, but they'll never be able to prove it.

OWN IT:

Excuse me. I am so sorry. I'll open a window.

In a car

DISOWN IT:

What a funny-sounding horn!

OWN IT:

What? The air freshener
tree ran out of smell…

In a long-term relationship

OWN IT:

I was just trying to blow you a kiss,
but it came out the wrong end.

In Spain

OWN IT:

¡Discúlpame me tiré un tiro!

In an elevator

DISOWN IT:

Who farted? That is just
wrong on so many levels!

OWN IT:

That fart was epic on so many levels!

In high school

DISOWN IT:

Someone is getting expelled!

In kindergarten

DISOWN IT:

Whoever smelt it, dealt it!

OWN IT:

uncontrollable giggling

In a hot air balloon

DISOWN IT:

That hot air? It's the balloon, obviously!

OWN IT:

I was just trying to help, it seemed like we were running out of gas.

If you have a dog

DISOWN IT:

Blame the dog. Always
blame the dog.

OWN IT:

My farts smell just like the dog's.

If you have a cat

DISOWN IT:

Blame the cat. Always blame the cat.

In private

DISOWN IT:

Someone tooted!

OWN IT:

Whispers to self: "I'm a private tutor."

Eating beans

OWN IT:

These too shall pass.

In a bar, trying to flirt with that cute girl

DISOWN IT:

Did you just fart? Because you blew me away!

40

At the zoo

DISOWN IT:

It was an elephant!

OWN IT:

All the animals were doing it!

With your kids

DISOWN IT:

Which one of you let one rip?

OWN IT:

Better out than in, I always say!

When you're a teacher

DISOWN IT:

Don't say anything. The kids will start blaming each other.

OWN IT:

Make it a science lesson: You see, class, I farted because there's bacteria in my large intestine to help digest food.

In a bathtub

DISOWN IT:

It was the Jacuzzi jets!

OWN IT:

I was just trying to make
it a Jacuzzi tub!

While whale watching

DISOWN IT:

There she blows! ...it was the whale.

OWN IT:

I was just trying to do my
best whale impression!

At a funeral

DISOWN IT:

Wow, it sure smells like a
dead corpse in here.

In a club

DISOWN IT:

Screaming: THAT WAS AN
INTENSE BASS DROP!

OWN IT:

What? I couldn't wait for the
bass to drop, so I did it myself.

When someone sneaks up on you

OWN IT:

You scared the farts right out of me!

During game night

OWN IT:

What can I say? I'm a competitive farter.

At a cheese shop

DISOWN IT:

Who's cutting cheese in here?

OWN IT:

Start actually cutting cheese:
I'm cutting the cheese.

In a fancy place amongst fancy people

DISOWN IT:

Some people…

During a debate

OWN IT:
Fart again. Then say: That's right, I doubled-down on that fart, because I meant to.

At a concert

DISOWN IT:

It's the tuba!

OWN IT:

Did you hear that butt trumpet solo?

In the library

OWN IT:

Whispering: I was shushing you
with my butt. Shhhhhh...

At a birthday party

DISOWN IT:

A balloon deflated…

OWN IT:

Party? I thought this was
a birthday farty!

When you're near a horse

DISOWN IT:

It was the horse, of course.

Running a marathon

DISOWN IT:

Say nothing and run FASTER!

OWN IT:

Pretend like you're a rocket
and run super fast like it's
propelling you forward.

At the beach

OWN IT:
SHART!

During a good laugh

DISOWN IT:

Someone is laughing out
of the wrong end!

OWN IT:

You know what they say?
Happiness comes from within,
and I'm just so full of happiness
that a little had to come out.

At a job interview

DISOWN IT:

I didn't fart. What you heard was the sound of you realizing that I'm the right man for the job.

OWN IT:

No sir, I didn't fart. What you smell is the smell of success.

In French

DISOWN IT:

*C'est toi qui a pété ? Franchement,
tu pourrais t'excuser !*

At the office

DISOWN IT:

It was the chair! The chair!

At a gas station

OWN IT:

At least this is some gas
I CAN afford!

In a daycare

DISOWN IT:

Diaper check time!

OWN IT:

What? The kids were doing it!

At a farmers market

DISOWN IT:

Wow! Those Brussels sprouts are REALLY fragrant, huh?

In church

DISOWN IT:

Holy shart! Who farted?

In someone else's house

DISOWN IT:

I think you might have a sewage leak.

When you're a parent

DISOWN IT:

Blame the kids!

OWN IT:

My farts are like kids: I'm proud of mine, but disgusted by yours.

When you're SUPER comfortable with your significant other

DISOWN IT:

I'm glad you feel comfortable enough to fart in front of me now.

OWN IT:

Pull the covers over both of you, and yell, "Dutch oven!"

On Halloween

OWN IT:

Farts are the ghosts of the
food we eat! Boo!

During sex

DISOWN IT:
Moan REALLY loudly while
you're letting it out. Trust
us, no one will notice.

OWN IT:
That's just what my big O
sounds like ¯_(ツ)_/¯

In detention

OWN IT:

I'm detained, but at least my gas is free! Free at last!

During a movie

DISOWN IT:

Say nothing. Fart during an explosion.

OWN IT:

Exclaim loudly, "Mmm, this popcorn smells good!" Everyone will take a big whiff.

When you're a clown

DISOWN IT:

Does it smell funny in here?

OWN IT:

Sorry, my butt made a funny!

On Easter

DISOWN IT:

It was the Easter Bunny!

or

Clearly, the eggs have gone rotten!

When you're trying to be ladylike

DISOWN IT:

That wasn't a fart, I just whispered in my undies.

OWN IT:

Goodness me, I'm so gassy!

During a nightmare

OWN IT:

Scream: I had to release a demon!

On Christmas

DISOWN IT:

I think the eggnog has gone bad.

OWN IT:

My colon has a present for you!

or

Jingle smells, jingle smells,
jingle all the way!

On the moon

DISOWN IT:

It smells bad because the moon is made of cheese, obviously!

OWN IT:

That's one small stinker for man, one giant toot for mankind!

In the woods

DISOWN IT:
Who's cranking a chainsaw?
or
I think I hear a lumberjack
cranking a chainsaw!

OWN IT:
If there's no one else around to
hear it, did it even make a sound?

During a massage

DISOWN IT:

Uhh…that was the table.

OWN IT:

What can I say? You're really working the kinks out…of my colon.

In art class

DISOWN IT:

Wait, is this not f(art) class?

OWN IT:

A fart? No, it's art. It's my colon's great masterpiece.

At a farm

OWN IT:

What? They said the crops
needed to be dusted.

During a magic show

DISOWN IT:

Please excuse my assistant!

OWN IT:

Watch closely as I turn these beans from a solid to a gas!

In science class.

DISOWN IT:

Who's producing methane in here?

OWN IT:

Behold! I have organically produced methane!

In New York City

DISOWN IT:

Blame anyone in your
immediate vicinity.

OWN IT:

Hey, watch it! I'm fartin' ova here!

At the bank

OWN IT:

Now I have gas money!

On a train

DISOWN IT:
It was the horn!

OWN IT:
I'm my best train
impression, "toot toot!"

On a plane

DISOWN IT:

There's clearly a gassy baby in here.

OWN IT:

I couldn't help it! I was
under pressure!

During yoga class

OWN IT:

You told me to exhale, but you didn't say out of which end!

At the dinner table

DISOWN IT:

Blame Mom's broccoli.

or

Blame a sibling.

If you're a snake charmer

DISOWN IT:

That hiss you heard? It was my snakes!

OWN IT:

Listen to my snake impression!

When you're a dad

OWN IT:

I'm the world's greatest farter…I mean, father!

Near a pond

DISOWN IT:

Who stepped on a duck?

OWN IT:

Sorry, my butt quacked.

When you see a shooting star

OWN IT:

A fart is a wish your butt makes.

When you're a ninja

DISOWN IT:

You're off the hook. Your farts are silent but deadly, so anyone who may have smelled them is dead. R.I.P.

In Las Vegas

OWN IT:

Winner, winner! Someone
had beans for dinner!

When people turn around

OWN IT:

Did I win *The Voice*?!

In the hospital

OWN IT:

Did you have a fart attack?

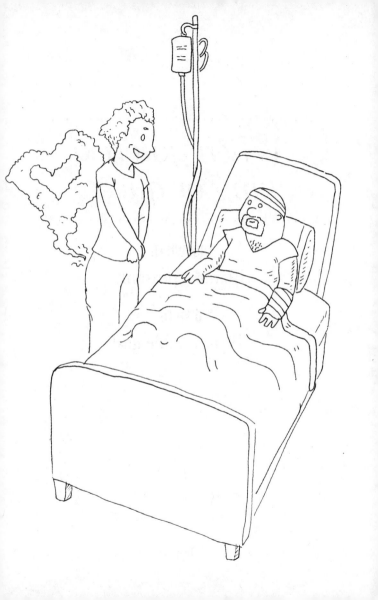

When you're a king or queen

DISOWN IT:

Blame a peasant.

OWN IT:

'Twas a noble gas!

When you're performing Shakespeare

OWN IT:

Men at some time are masters of
their farts:
The fault is not in our
stars, but in ourselves.

When you fart so bad that it's offensive

DISOWN IT:

I'm a-gass-ed! Who farted?

OWN IT:

I'm sorry, I'm even a-gass-ed
at myself!

If you're a chicken or a turkey

DISOWN IT:

You're foul.

OWN IT:

I'm fowl.

Conclusion

Happy farting, folks!

About the Illustrator

MIKE BECK is an illustrator and graphic designer living in Bridgeport, Connecticut. He enjoys sandwiches and woodburning. One time, during a dreadful snowstorm, he successfully cuddled the hypothermia out of a complete stranger. He has never once farted.